THE BIG WHY

THE WONDERS OF NUMBERS

BY GRACE TOGUN

ILLUSTRATED BY MANGALIK SOBHAKAR

THE BIG WHY: THE WONDERS OF NUMBERS
Book 1 in a Series of 5

First Published by BeGenio Publishing in the United Kingdom

www.easymathskills.com,
info@easymathskills.com

"Dad, can we go home yet?" asked James, glancing at his watch.
"We have been out for 10 hours!"
His father looked at James in surprise. "10 hours?" he asked.
James held up his Superman wristwatch for his Dad to see.
"See here?" he said. "It says 10 hours."

It was a beautiful Saturday morning. The sun was shining hot and bright, and James was out with his father, walking in the Barsby Town Centre.
James' father shook his head. "No, son. It says 10 o'clock."
James tilted his head in confusion. "Isn't that the same, Daddy?" he asked.
His father took James' hand in his own.
"Look at the watch. We left home at 8 o'clock, right?" James nodded.

"And what time is it now?" asked his father.
"10 o'clock," murmured James.
"Yes!" said his father, "so, we have been out from 8 to 9,
and then from 9 to 10," explained his father.
"How many hours is that, James?"
"Two!" chirped James.
"That's right!" cheered his father.
"And what if we stay out for another hour?"
"Then we will be out for 3 hours!"
said James. "That's correct!

That reminds me of a special pattern. It's a sequence!" said Dad in excitement, his eyes lighting up. "Do you know what we call this pattern?

"What do we call it, Daddy?" asked James curiously.

"We call it the Fibonacci Sequence," explained Dad. "We add the last two numbers to make the next number, and it forms a pattern. It is like a series of numbers."

James' eyes' widened. "Wow!" said James. "The Fibon what?

"The Fi-bon-a-cci sequence son." Dad said with a grin.
"Yep." said Dad. "so the first two of the series start from 0 and 1 and the next one is 1."
"Why? Because the first two numbers of the series are 0 and 1.
So when you add 0 and 1 together.
what do you get?" asked James' father."1!" said James.
"Good! What's the next number of
the Fibonacci series?" asked his father.
"1 + 1 = 2!" answered James.
"Fabulous!" said Dad. "And the next
will be 1 + 2 = 3." Dad added.

They walked a couple of minutes further, past the park, and saw three trees next to each other near the swings and slides.

"Let's sit down for a minute James," said his father. "Let me tell you a little story.

They sat on a bench beside the trees.

"A very long time ago in the Thirteenth-Century, a man named Leonardo Fibonacci discovered that important number sequence," Dad continued.

"Thirteenth-Century?" James asked.

"Yes," said Dad. "That's about 700 years ago."

"Seven hundred?" exclaimed James, his eyes still wide open and brimming with excitement. James could not believe what he was hearing. The numbers sounded so big!

"Yes, son," said his father. "Leonardo discovered a simple sequence of numbers, which is what we call the Fibonacci Sequence or Fibonacci Series."

"For some mysterious reason, James, this sequence of numbers seems to appear in a wide number of places in real-life, in our natural world," continued his father. "In sea life like in sea shells, on land, in fruits, in many trees, in plants, in flowers, tiny living things, big living things and in lots of places everywhere!" "You can see this in this tree," said Dad pointing to the tree in the middle. "Look at this tree, it starts with the branch at the bottom, then branches out into two, then into three..." Dad paused looking at James. "Can you see how many branches the tree has next?"

"Five!" James squealed with excitement.
"Can you see where it goes into?" asked Dad.
"Eight. Eight. Daddy!" squealed James. "I see eight!"
"Correct!" Dad said. "Well done. son! We can actually draw a spiral around the branching sequence of that tree."
"Look. James." Dad drew in the air as if he was drawing on the tree. following the beginning of each branch in a circular motion with his hands.

"Can you start to see Math in our everyday Life, James?" asked his father.
"Yes, Daddy!" replied James.
"Do you remember when I told you that Math is everywhere?" asked James' father.
When the boy nodded, his father continued.
"There is a saying by a famous Mathematician that says "Numbers rulethe Universe!" said Dad.
"Woah!" exclaimed James. "Numbers rule the Universe? Like... the Whole Wide World?" said James, unable to contain his excitement further!

James stood up and Leaped from excitement, he could hardly sit still!
"Yes son, because Math is everywhere! In buildings, in dance steps, door numbers, how hot or how cold something is, on Leaves, in the music we play, in form of shapes on traffic cones and in sugar cubes," explained his father with a smile.

"Incredible!" James said, listening intently.

"It's even in buying and selling at the sweet shops and supermarkets I always take you and Laura too."

"What's his name, Daddy? I am going to tell my friends about him when school starts again!"

Dad thought for a moment... "Hmmm I can't remember right now but I will look it up for you, son, alright?"

"That's okay, Daddy," said James, "I can't wait to tell Ben about this when I get to school on Monday!"

James wanted to continue counting, but it was time to go now.

James could still not contain his excitement.
The pair of them walked towards a bookstore.
He could not even walk calmly anymore. James was skipping down the footpath. He could not believe there were numbers everywhere. He stared at Dad in amazement.
"Calm down now James," said Dad with a grin,
"What books would you like to buy?"

James picked out 3 books to buy. He handed them to his father.
Then as they were going to the counter, he found another book he wanted to buy.
He picked up that one and headed to the counter.
"How many books are you buying, James?" asked his father.
"I was buying 3 before," said James, "now I'm buying 1 more. So, 4 books!"
His father smiled. "That's right!"

Then his Dad pulled out another book from behind his back. "Here's 1 more."
"We had 4 books before. Now we have 1 more. How many are we going to buy?"
"5!" said James and his father ruffled his hair with a smile.
James said, "Ah I know! 3 books and 5 books are numbers in that sequence again!".

"Absolutely!" Dad replied.
Next, they went to a bakery to buy doughnuts.
James began counting the doughnuts on display
and inside the glass counter.
He wanted to see if he could find any patterns in the numbers.
James counted the display first. "That's 1 doughnut," he muttered.
James began counting the doughnuts in the middle. "1, 2, 3,"
he counted, "that makes 3."

To his right, he found 5 more doughnuts.
"That's 8 doughnuts!" he exclaimed."
His eyes lit up when he recognized the sequence of numbers.
"Dad!" he said excitedly, "Look, the Fibonacci Sequence!"
His father smiled. "You have learned the Fibonacci
Sequence quite well, son. I am proud of you!"

When they left the bookstore, they started looking at the buildings and could see several shapes within each building. "Look, James," Dad pointed at the building to their right. "A triangle at the top. That roof, then the bricks themselves are rectangles. Can you see any other shapes, James? " he asked.

"A square," James said. "That whole building is a square under the roof!"
"That's right," said Dad. "You are doing so well with this!"
James beamed. "Looking at these shapes and picking them out is so much fun, Dad!".
They walked past a man who was playing very loud music. James felt like dancing!

"Dad, Look! He's tapping three times first, and then when he turns he's tapping five times!".
Dad dropped a coin on the music man's tray which was Laid on a piece of cLoth. James
waLked very sLowLy, watching the number of times he was tapping each time.
"Come on then James, time to go," caLLed out Dad. James sped up to catch up with Dad.

They walked towards the exit. When they got to the car park, Dad told James to look at the car plates. One was X138JPD, and beside it was another car plate Y831ZZZ. Dad asked James to look at the numbers.
"What is common between those?" asked father.
"Oh! They have 7 number plate characters each," said James.
"And what else do you notice?" asked Dad.

James looked at the numbers more closely.
"Oh, I know!" said he. "They both have 3 numbers!"
"Yes, that's great! Well done, James!" praised Dad.
"Do you notice anything else?" he asked.
James thought for a while then shook his head.
"Have another look James," that's my challenge to you.
James stared at the car plate numbers again.
"I see it! They are Fibonacci numbers!"

"Yes!" and Dad kept staring.

"And," James squealed "the two numbers in each car plate are the reverse of each other?"

"BRAVO!" Dad clapped. "That's it, son! You've noticed another pattern in those numbers, in two ways!"

James gave Dad a friendly hi-five! "That's so true! Daddy!"

"I'm going to tell you one more thing at home about these plate numbers... I bet you will find it very exciting. It's my favorite number trick!" said Dad.

"Oh, Dad," said James, "I can't wait to go home! I also can't wait to tell mom and Laura all about this and how Math is linked to our lives!" When they reached home, Mom was doing laundry. James rushed in. "Mom, I need to tell you something!" he exclaimed. James started telling mom all about his time spent out that day with Dad while mom was sorting the clothes.

She put 3 of James' shirts in the washing machine, then added 5 pairs of shorts. "8," counted James. "There it is again!". "What," said Laura and mom at the same time. "The Fibonacci sequence!" James said. Laura seemed very confused. "The what?"

James sat down with mom and Laura and explained the Fibonacci sequence of numbers to them.

James looked back at his father who was waiting to show him a special trick.

"I still need to practice some numbers," he told his father.

He raced after his mom as she went to the kitchen and started adding ingredients to make a mix for a cake.
"Where are you going, James?" asked his father.
"To practice!" James called over his shoulder.
Dad waited patiently.

Suddenly, James remembered what Dad said he was going to show him about the car plates' numbers trick! "Wait a minute, Dad!" James stopped in his tracks! "What about that number trick you said you will show me?" "Aha," said Dad. "I had wondered whether you would remember or not! Good lad! Go do the baking with mom first and I will then sit you children down and show you some magic this evening."

"Magic? Okay, Dad. That's cool!"James could not believe what a fun day he was having today! And it was all because of Math!

Later that day, Dad sat down with mom and the children and started to tell them something so amazing.

"Oh my!" Laura said, her eyes popping. "Is that real Dad"?

TO BE CONTINUED...

Manufactured by Amazon.ca
Bolton, ON

55901378R00021